Happy Easter
Much love,
Aunt Cathy
2020

Simon of Cyrene
and the Legend
of the
Easter Egg

Written by Terri DeGezelle

Illustrated by Gabhor Utomo

Pauline
BOOKS & MEDIA
Boston

Library of Congress Cataloging-in-Publication Data

Names: DeGezelle, Terri, 1955- author. | Utomo, Gabhor, illustrator.
Title: Simon of Cyrene and the legend of the Easter egg / written by Terri
 DeGezelle ; illustrated by Gabhor Utomo.
Description: Boston : Pauline Books & Media, 2017.
Identifiers: LCCN 2016028405| ISBN 9780819890702 (hardcover) | ISBN
 0819890707 (hardcover)
Subjects: LCSH: Simon, of Cyrene--Juvenile literature. | Simon, of
 Cyrene--Legends. | Easter eggs--Juvenile literature.
Classification: LCC BS2520.S7 D44 2017 | DDC 232.96--dc23
LC record available at https://lccn.loc.gov/2016028405

Scripture quotations contained herein are from the *New Revised Standard Version Bible: Catholic Edition*, copyright © 1989, 1993, Division of Christian Education of the National Council of the Churches of Christ in the United States of America. Used by permission. All rights reserved.

Design by Mary Joseph Peterson, FSP

Illustrated by Gabhor Utomo

"P" and PAULINE are registered trademarks of the Daughters of St. Paul.

Published by Pauline Books & Media, 50 Saint Paul's Avenue, Boston, MA 02130–3491

Printed in China

TLEE NAPCHIDONJN9-291000002 9070-7

www.pauline.org

Pauline Books & Media is the publishing house of the Daughters of St. Paul, an international congregation of women religious serving the Church with the communications media.

1 2 3 4 5 6 7 8 9   21 20 19 18 17

To my parents,
Richard and Kathleen Longenecker,
who taught by action how to reach out to others
just as Simon did.

They compelled a passerby,
who was coming in from the country to carry his cross;
it was Simon of Cyrene,
the father of Alexander and Rufus.

Mark 15:21

"Pray our eggs bring a good price at market,"
Simon said to his wife, Ruth.

"Lord knows we need the money. I'm sure you will
find buyers," Ruth answered. "Many people will be in
Jerusalem for the Passover feast."

Simon hugged his two sons, Alexander and Rufus,
goodbye. "Help your mother while I'm gone." Simon
took his basket of eggs wrapped in cloth and began
the long walk toward the city.

   As he entered Jerusalem, Simon heard a crowd
shouting angrily. People lined both sides of the road.
Simon came closer and saw a man dragging a cross.
People in the crowd spit and threw stones at the man
as he stumbled.

   "What has this man done?" Simon wondered
aloud.

A young man standing next to him overheard Simon. "His name is Jesus, and he's done nothing to deserve this," the man explained. "Jesus is the Messiah."

"I've heard people speak about him," Simon responded after introducing himself. "You think he's the savior God promised to send?"

"I'm John. I've followed Jesus for the last three years. I have seen the miracles he's worked. He is not a criminal!" John said. "But now, they are going to kill him—"

Two hands gripped Simon's shoulders from behind. "He's already fallen once, and this is taking too long. *You* carry the cross for him!" a Roman soldier yelled.

Simon had just enough time to hand his basket to
John before the soldier shoved him forward.

I'm afraid of these soldiers, but John said Jesus is innocent, Simon thought. He had heard about Jesus, the rabbi from Nazareth who always reached out to help people. Simon looked at Jesus' crown of thorns. Blood and sweat soaked his tunic. Jesus was suffering greatly. This man, who had helped so many people, now needed help. Moved by compassion, Simon prayed quietly as he neared Jesus. "God, help me to help Jesus like he's helped so many other people."

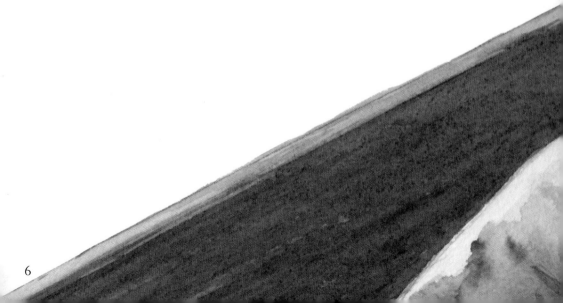

Simon gently lifted the cross off Jesus' shoulders and said, "I'll help you as much as I can." Then Simon began following Jesus up the hill.

The road to Calvary was long, and splinters from
the wooden beam dug painfully into Simon's shoulder.
Jesus grew weaker with each step. Along the way Jesus
fell two more times. Simon watched as the crowds
jeered and the soldiers shouted.

When they reached Calvary, a soldier pushed
Simon aside and shouted, "You're no longer needed.
Be gone with you!"

Simon saw John standing nearby with two women.
They watched as Jesus was nailed to the cross. Then,
as Jesus hung on the cross, Simon heard him say
to one of the women, "Woman, behold your son."
Looking at John, Jesus said, "Behold, your mother."

He's even taking care of other people as he's dying,
Simon thought with amazement.

After Jesus died, Simon helped men carry Jesus'
body to the tomb. A woman who had stood at the
foot of the cross approached Simon. "Thank you for
helping Jesus," she said. "I'm Mary Magdalene, one of
his followers." Pointing to the older weeping woman,
she added, "And that's his mother, Mary."

After Jesus was buried, Mary, the mother of Jesus, put her hand on Simon's shoulder. "Simon, it's too late to find a place to stay," she said. "Please, come spend the night with us."

The next day, Simon listened as Jesus' mother and friends shared memories of Jesus.

"Jesus fed five thousand hungry people with only five loaves of bread and two fish!" Peter remembered.

"Jesus said he loved all of us as brothers and sisters," another disciple told Simon. "He washed our feet. He told us that we could show our love for him by loving and serving others."

"What else did Jesus say?" Simon asked.

Mary Magdalene responded, "Jesus said that he would suffer and die, but after three days he would rise again."

"That's right!" John said. "Jesus also said that we'd feel sorrow when he went away from us, but that we'd see him again and rejoice! I wonder . . ."

Do they really believe that Jesus might come back to life? Simon wondered.

Early the next morning, Simon prepared to go home. Suddenly, Mary Magdalene rushed in, joyfully shouting, "I have seen the Lord! Jesus is alive!"

John and Peter immediately ran to the tomb.
Everyone else in the house listened to Mary
Magdalene's story.

Simon opened the door when he heard Peter and
John running back up the hill.

"It's true! Jesus is risen!" John announced.

"When we got to the tomb," Peter explained,
breathless, "there was nothing but a few cloths!"

After celebrating with the others, Simon picked up his basket of eggs and turned to John. "I didn't sell any eggs," Simon said. "But I'm so glad I spent this time with you. I can't wait to get home and tell Ruth and my boys about Jesus!"

After arriving home, Simon told his family all he knew about Jesus. Then Simon picked up his basket of eggs. The cloth slipped off. The eggs were no longer white!

"This must be a gift from Jesus!" Simon said. He lifted a rosy-pink egg. "It's the color of the sunrise this morning when Jesus rose from the dead. And here is an egg as blue as the Sea of Galilee that Jesus walked on. This egg is green, like the hillside where he fed five thousand people. Look—a red egg, the color of Jesus' blood poured out in love for you and me. And lastly, this purple egg is the color of royalty. Jesus truly is the King who loves and serves those in need." Simon looked at his family and smiled. "Now we must follow him and do the same."

Simon of Cyrene

Simon of Cyrene is mentioned in the Gospels of Matthew, Mark, and Luke. He is also mentioned in the fifth station of the Stations of the Cross: Simon helps Jesus carry his cross. The story you have just read about Simon's eggs changing colors is based on an old German legend.

We don't know a lot about Simon. What we *do* know is that he was coming to Jerusalem at the same time Jesus was carrying the cross. We also know that after Simon met Jesus face to face, his life changed.

Simon's hometown of Cyrene is located in a lush valley in the highlands of Libya, in northern Africa. Historical sources tell us there was a Roman colony in Cyrene, and that a number of Jews lived there. Jewish Cyrenians often came to Jerusalem on pilgrimages to celebrate festivals.

According to Christian tradition, Simon's sons, Rufus and Alexander, became missionaries when they grew up. Some believe they held places of honor and authority in the early Christian community in Rome.

Prayer *for* Courage *and* Compassion

Dear Jesus,

Thank you for loving me so much you were willing to die on the cross.

I want to be like Simon, who helped you when you needed it most.

Provide me with strength to help those in need and show compassion for those who are hurting.

Show me how to spread your love and mercy to others.

Give me the courage to do this even when I am afraid.

May everyone experience the joy of your Resurrection.

Amen.

Author and photographer **Terri DeGezelle** was born Theresa Ann Longenecker on October 1, the feast day of Saint Thérèse of Lisieux, "The Little Flower." The Sisters of the Sorrowful Mother operated the hospital where she was born and the sister in the delivery room wrote the baby's name as Theresa on the birth certificate before her parents could protest. Sister said, "Saint Thérèse is too good of a saint to waste by not using her name." Having a grandmother and aunt named Theresa, the new baby went by Terri.

Terri has published more than sixty children's nonfiction titles as well as 100 magazine articles and several photos in national publications.

Terri is a presenter at young writers' and young artists' conferences around the Upper Midwest. She enjoys sharing her skills during school visits and inspiring students to follow their dreams while being the best they can be. Terri's passions include attending daily Mass, praying the Rosary, reading, writing, spending time with her adult children, playing with her grandchildren, and photographing the world around her.

Gabhor Utomo was born in Indonesia and moved to California to pursue his passion for art. In the spring of 2003, he graduated from the Academy of Art University in San Francisco. Since then, Gabhor has worked as a freelance illustrator on a number of children's books. The first book he illustrated, *Kai's Journey to Gold Mountain*, is a story about a young Chinese immigrant on Angel Island.

Gabhor's works have won numerous awards from local and national art organizations. His painting of Senator Milton Marks is part of a permanent collection at the California State Building in downtown San Francisco.

Gabhor now lives in Portland, Oregon, with his wife, Dina, and their twin girls. To see more of his beautiful illustrations, please visit gabhorutomo.com.

Tales and Legends from

Pauline kids

The 3 Trees

Adapted by Gabriel Ringlet
Illustrated by Daniella Oh

The Little Lost Lamb

Written and Illustrated
by Geri Berger Haines

the QUEEN & the CROSS

The Story of
Saint Helen

Written by
Cornelia Mary Bilinsky
Illustrated by
Rebecca Stuhff

SANTA'S Secret Story

Written by
Cornelia Mary Bilinsky
Illustrated by
Candace Camling

The Saint who Fought the Dragon

The Story of
Saint George

Written by
Cornelia Mary Bilinsky
Illustrated by
Theresa Brandon

Spider's Gift

A Christmas Story

Written by
Geraldine Ann Marshall
Illustrated by
Rebecca Sorge

Who are the Daughters of St. Paul?

We are Catholic sisters. Our mission is to be like Saint Paul and tell everyone about Jesus! There are so many ways for people to communicate with each other. We want to use all of them so everyone will know how much God loves us. We do this by printing books (you're holding one!), making radio shows, singing, helping people at our bookstores, using the internet, and in many other ways.

VISIT OUR WEB SITE AT WWW.PAULINE.ORG

auline
BOOKS & MEDIA

The Daughters of St. Paul operate book and media centers
at the following addresses. Visit, call, or write the one nearest you today,
or find us at www.paulinestore.org.

CALIFORNIA
3908 Sepulveda Blvd, Culver City, CA 90230 — 310-397-8676
3250 Middlefield Road, Menlo Park, CA 94025 — 650-369-4230

FLORIDA
145 SW 107th Avenue, Miami, FL 33174 — 305-559-6715

HAWAII
1143 Bishop Street, Honolulu, HI 96813 — 808-521-2731

ILLINOIS
172 North Michigan Avenue, Chicago, IL 60601 — 312-346-4228

LOUISIANA
4403 Veterans Memorial Blvd, Metairie, LA 70006 — 504-887-7631

MASSACHUSETTS
885 Providence Hwy, Dedham, MA 02026 — 781-326-5385

MISSOURI
9804 Watson Road, St. Louis, MO 63126 — 314-965-3512

NEW YORK
64 West 38th Street, New York, NY 10018 — 212-754-1110

SOUTH CAROLINA
243 King Street, Charleston, SC 29401 — 843-577-0175

TEXAS
Currently no book center; for parish exhibits or outreach evangelization,
contact: 210-569-0500 or SanAntonio@paulinemedia.com
or P.O. Box 761416, San Antonio, TX 78245

VIRGINIA
1025 King Street, Alexandria, VA 22314 — 703-549-3806

CANADA
3022 Dufferin Street, Toronto, ON M6B 3T5 — 416-781-9131

Smile
God loves you